CENGAGE Learning

Drama for Students, Volume 21

Project Editor: Anne Marie Hacht

Editorial: Michelle Kazensky, Ira Mark Milne, Timothy Sisler **Rights Acquisition and Management**: Margaret Abendroth, Edna Hedblad, Jacqueline Key, Mari Masalin-Cooper **Manufacturing**: Rhonda Williams

Imaging: Lezlie Light, Mike Logusz, Kelly A. Quin **Product Design**: Pamela A. E. Galbreath

Product Manager: Meggin Condino

For more information, contact
Gale, an imprint of Cengage Learning
27500 Drake Rd.
Farmington Hills, MI 48331-3535
Or you can visit our Internet site at

individual does not imply endorsement of the editors or publisher. Errors brought to the attention of the publisher and verified to the satisfaction of the publisher will be corrected in future editions.

ISBN 0-7876-6818-4
ISSN 1094-9232

Printed in the United States of America
10 9 8 7 6 5 4 3 2 1

Tamburlaine the Great

Christopher Marlowe 1590

Introduction

In 1587, Christopher Marlowe, William Shakespeare's contemporary and one of the star playwrights of the English Renaissance, produced a daring and thrilling play focusing on the triumphs of a Tartar conqueror. Famous for adeptly incorporating the style of blank verse (unrhymed iambic pentameter) into English drama, the play was so popular that Marlowe was compelled to write a sequel including Tamburlaine's and his wife's deaths. Together, the plays became known as *Tamburlaine the Great*. Poetically captivating, as forceful and powerful as Tamburlaine the character, Marlowe's verse in these works marks a major shift from the conventional, low comic style of other Renaissance works. The plays are not a straightforward glorification of Tamburlaine's violent conquests, since Marlowe frequently highlights his protagonist's excessive brutality and hubris, or excessive pride. However, their directness and eloquence make it difficult not to admire Tamburlaine, both for his rhetorical power and his lifelike animation.

Alongside Tamburlaine's ceaseless conquests and their implications about war and politics run more general themes of desire, ambition, and power. Marlowe uses his portrayal of Tamburlaine's capture, betrothal, marriage, and ultimate loss of his wife Zenocrate, the daughter of the Egyptian "soldan," or sultan, to highlight these themes in another context, questioning the true nature of his hero's romantic passion. The plays also comment on ideas of fatherhood and masculinity by way of Tamburlaine's expectations of his sons, including his cruel treatment and murder of his son Calyphas, whom he considers a coward. Marlowe develops all of these themes through his skillful and unique use of language, which is why he is considered perhaps the most important stylistic innovator of the period. Originally published in 1590, the plays are now available in modern editions with notes and introductory material, such as the New Mermaid edition, *Tamburlaine the Great: Parts I and II*, published by Ernest Benn Limited in 1971.

Author Biography

Born in Canterbury, England on February 6, 1564, Marlowe was the son of a shoemaker. He attended King's School in Canterbury and was awarded a scholarship to Cambridge University, where he studied dialectics. Because of a number of mysterious absences from college, Marlowe was in danger of not receiving his master of arts degree. But Queen Elizabeth's Privy Council intervened with a letter stating that he had been in the queen's service and not, as was the rumor, part of a Catholic conspiracy in Rheims, France. In fact, many historians believe Marlowe was a spy of the queen's advisor Sir Francis Walsingham, which would explain his powerful connections and the company of spies and politicians with whom he associated.

In any case, Marlowe moved to London in 1587 with his degree and began writing in earnest. Before the year was out, the first part of *Tamburlaine the Great* had been performed to great success, and Marlowe produced its sequel in the following year. *Tamburlaine the Great* was the only one of Marlowe's works to be published during his lifetime, but he wrote and produced at least five more plays, including *Edward II*, a sophisticated play about the downfall of a weak king and his treacherous usurper Mortimer, and *Dr. Faustus*, in which Faustus sells his soul to the devil in exchange for power and knowledge. Before writing these plays, however, Marlowe translated poetry by the ancient Romans Ovid and Lucan. Later, he translated (with some additions of his own witty innovations) the ancient Greek poem *Hero and Leander*.

While living in London, Marlowe associated with the dramatist Thomas Kyd and the poet Thomas Watson. In 1589, Marlowe and Watson were briefly imprisoned for their roles in the homicide of a publican. In the subsequent years, Marlowe was involved in several other scuffles and legal disputes. In 1593, Kyd accused him of authoring several heretical papers that had been discovered in Kyd's room. Marlowe appeared before the queen's Privy Council, which was the normal course for a gentlemen; it was afforded to Marlowe, most likely, because of his continued associations with powerful politicians, but there is no evidence that they examined him. Shortly afterwards, on May 30, 1593, Marlowe spent all day with Ingram Frizer, a known operative of the powerful Walsingham family, and two other men at a meeting house in Deptford, near London. Frizer stabbed Marlowe above the right eye and killed him. The reasons for the attack and murder remain a mystery. Frizer was pardoned of the murder within a month.

Plot Summary

Part 1, Acts 1–2

Tamburlaine the Great begins with a prologue declaring that, unlike the silly wordplay of previous literature, this play will feature the "high astounding" words and actions of a conqueror. Act 1 then opens with the king of Persia, Mycetes, complaining to his brother Cosroe of a band of outlaws led by a "Scythian" shepherd named Tamburlaine. Scythians would technically have lived north and northeast of the Black Sea, but Marlowe uses the term interchangeably with "Tartar," which signifies the area of East Asia controlled by Mongol tribes. Cosroe criticizes his brother for being a weak and foolish king, and Mycetes instructs his chief captain Theridamas to kill Tamburlaine and his band before they enter Persia. Then, two Persian lords inform Cosroe of widespread unrest and offer him the crown, which Cosroe accepts.

Act 1, scene 2 introduces Tamburlaine, who has captured the Egyptian princess Zenocrate and is declaring his love for her. Theridamas arrives with one thousand soldiers, compared to Tamburlaine's five hundred, but Tamburlaine convinces Theridamas in a parlay to join his side. In act 2, Cosroe joins with Tamburlaine to overthrow his brother. When Mycetes hears of this, his lord

Meander forms a plan to throw gold on the field in order to distract soldiers, whom he considers to be greedy thieves. Tamburlaine encounters Mycetes attempting to hide his crown in a hole; Tamburlaine tells Mycetes that he will not steal his crown yet, but take it when he wins the battle. After Tamburlaine and Cosroe conquer Mycetes's army, Cosroe departs for Persepolis, the capitol. Tamburlaine decides to challenge Cosroe to a battle for the Persian crown. Tamburlaine triumphs and Cosroe dies, cursing Tamburlaine and Theridamas.

Part 1, Acts 3–5

In act 3, scene 1, the Turkish Emperor Bajazeth discusses with his subsidiary kings their siege of Constantinople, which was then held by Christians. He warns Tamburlaine not to enter Africa or "Graecia," which included much of the Balkan peninsula, then under Turkish control. In the next scene, Tamburlaine overhears the Median, or Iranian, Lord Agydas urge Zenocrate to disdain Tamburlaine's suit, but Zenocrate stresses that she wants to be his wife. Tamburlaine surprises them, and Agydas stabs himself to avoid torture. Act 3 concludes with Tamburlaine's victory over the Turks and Tamburlaine making slaves of Bajazeth and his wife Zabina.

Zenocrate's father, the "soldan," or sultan of Egypt, opens act 4 by vowing to stop Tamburlaine's advances upon Egypt with the help of the king of Arabia, who was Zenocrate's betrothed before

Tamburlaine kidnapped her. Tamburlaine and Zenocrate then humiliate and torture Bajazeth and Zabina. Tamburlaine vows to overtake Egypt despite his wife's plea to pity her father. In act 5, the governor of Damascus, besieged by Tamburlaine's army, sends a group of virgins to plead for mercy, but Tamburlaine has them slaughtered and hoisted on the city walls. When Tamburlaine goes to fight the soldan and the king of Arabia, Bajazeth and Zabina kill themselves by beating out their brains. Zenocrate finds them and is dismayed by their and her people's blood on Tamburlaine's hands. After the king of Arabia dies and Tamburlaine wins the battle, sparing the soldan's life and actually giving him more territory than before, Tamburlaine crowns Zenocrate queen of Persia.

Part 2, Acts 1–3

Orcanes, the king of "Natolia," or Anatolia, the region east of the Bosporus in present-day Turkey, and Sigismond of Hungary begin act 1 by swearing to uphold a truce, while Tamburlaine advances on Anatolia from Egypt. Bajazeth's son Callapine, who is Tamburlaine's prisoner in Egypt, then convinces his jailer Almeda to help him escape, promising him a kingdom. Meanwhile, Tamburlaine instructs his three sons on the arts of war; he harasses Calyphas, the son not inclined to fight, for being a coward. Tamburlaine meets Theridamas, Techelles, and Usumcasane, and they prepare to march on Natolia.

In act 2, Sigismond agrees to break his vow

with Orcanes and attack the Natolian army while Orcanes is preparing to engage Tamburlaine. Orcanes wins the battle, however, attributing the victory partly to Christ, since Sigismond broke his vow to the Christian savior. Tamburlaine then discovers that Zenocrate is sick. Her physicians can do nothing to save her, and she dies. Act 3 begins with the crowning of Callapine as the Turkish emperor, and Callapine's vow to avenge his father's wrongs. Tamburlaine then burns down the town in which Zenocrate died, forbidding the world to rebuild it, and gives his sons a lesson in fortitude. Theridamas and Techelles march northward, where they sack Balsera, a town on the Natolian frontier. They capture its captain's wife, Olympia, after she burns her son's and husband's bodies. Tamburlaine and Usumcasane then parlay with Callapine and his subsidiary kings, threatening each other and boasting.

Part 2, Acts 4–5

Act 4, scene 1 reveals Tamburlaine's sons Amyras and Celebinus attempting to convince their brother Calyphas to fight, but Calyphas refuses. After Tamburlaine returns in triumph, he stabs Calyphas, calling him slothful and weak and ordering that the Turkish concubines bury him. In the next scene, Theridamas attempts to court Olympia, but she wishes to die and tricks him into stabbing her. Tamburlaine then rides in his chariot drawn by the former kings of "Soria," or Syria, and "Trebizon," or Trabzon, an area in the northeastern section of present-day Turkey, and tells his soldiers to rape the Turkish concubines.

Tamburlaine's next conquest is of Babylon. Since the governor refuses to yield the city, Tamburlaine has him hung in chains and shot. He then orders the kings of Trebizon and Soria hung, bridles Orcanes and Jerusalem on his coach, orders all Babylonian men, women, and children drowned, and commands that sacred Islamic books be burnt. Afterwards, Tamburlaine feels "distempered," and soon it becomes clear that Tamburlaine is deathly ill. En route to Persia, a messenger arrives to inform Tamburlaine that Callapine, who escaped from the battle in Natolia, has gathered a fresh army and means to attack. Tamburlaine scares them away, but he is too weak to pursue them. He retires to review his conquests and regret that he cannot conquer more. He then crowns his son Amyras, orders Zenocrate's hearse to be brought in, and dies.

Characters

Agydas

Agydas is the Median, or Iranian, lord traveling to Egypt with Zenocrate when Tamburlaine captures them. Tamburlaine overhears Agydas advising Zenocrate to resist the "vile and barbarous" Tamburlaine's advances. Agydas stabs himself to avoid torture.

Alcidamus

See King of Arabia

Almeda

Almeda is Callapine's jailer, whom Callapine convinces to release him by promising Almeda a kingdom in Turkey. Callapine does in fact give him a kingdom before battling with Tamburlaine, although Almeda will never rule it because Tamburlaine wins the battle.

Amyras

Tamburlaine's son and successor, who reluctantly accepts the crown while his father is dying, Amyras is a militaristic young man who idealizes his father. He revels in war, asking his father after they subdue the Turks whether they can release them and fight them again so that none may say it was a chance victory. However, as Amyras laments in the final lines of the play, he is no equal to Tamburlaine and will not be able to continue the glory of his reign.

Anippe

Anippe is Zenocrate's maid, whose right it is to treat the Turkish Empress Zabina as a servant after Tamburlaine subdues the Turkish armies.

Bajazeth

The emperor of Turkey in part 1, until Tamburlaine conquers his armies and makes him a slave, Bajazeth is a proud Islamic leader who ultimately beats his brains out on his cage rather than be subject to more humiliation and starvation. Bajazeth swears before his last battle to remove Tamburlaine's testicles and force him to draw his wife's chariot. While captive, Bajazeth frequently curses Tamburlaine, highlighting his most barbarous moments. Bajazeth's son Callapine extends the recurring theme of a bitter and vengeful enemy to Tamburlaine into part 2.

Bassoes

Now spelled "Bashaws" or "Pashas," a bassoe was the title given to Turkish officials. In the play, bassoes are servants of Bajazeth.

Callapine

Bajazeth's son and heir to the Turkish Empire, Callapine has dedicated his life to avenging his father's cruel treatment and to destroying Tamburlaine. Callapine is a cunning leader who manages to win over his jailer and escape from Tamburlaine's prison. Callapine also escapes from the battle that he loses to Tamburlaine, returning to attack Tamburlaine's army at the end of the play. Although Callapine is no match for Tamburlaine, he does manage to stay alive and unconquered throughout the play, completely committed to, as he puts it, "conquering the tyrant of the world." The implication is that he will return to haunt Amyras after Tamburlaine dies.

Calyphas

Calyphas is Tamburlaine's son, whom Tamburlaine murders after he refuses to fight in the battle against the Turks. Calyphas is somewhat weak and slothful, which Tamburlaine despises. But Calyphas is also simply uninterested in war; he is content to play cards and fantasize about women.

Captain of Balsera

Olympia's husband, the captain refuses to yield his hold to Techelles and Theridamas, and he is killed in the subsequent invasion.

Casane

See Usumcasane

Celebinus

Tamburlaine's son, Celebinus, is a forceful young man who emulates his father.

Cosroe

Brother to the Mycetes, king of Persia, Cosroe usurps his brother's title with Tamburlaine's help. Cosroe worries about the state of the empire under his brother's ineffectual rule, and he determines at the bequest of several Persian lords to take the crown and rule more wisely. Although Cosroe is not as weak as his brother, he is naive enough to leave Tamburlaine and his companions with all of their soldiers after they win the battle for the Persian crown, and Tamburlaine quickly challenges him to battle and triumphs.

Frederick

A peer of Hungary, Frederick persuades Sigismund to break his vow of peace with Orcanes.

Gazellus

The viceroy, or ruler with the mandate of a king, of the Turkish territory of Byron, Gazellus is an ally and advisor to Orcanes.

Governor of Babylon

Stubborn and unyielding, the governor of Babylon refuses to allow Tamburlaine inside his city. When he is conquered and under threat of death, however, he attempts to bribe Tamburlaine by telling him where a stockpile of gold is hidden. Tamburlaine has him hanged nevertheless.

Governor of Damascus

The governor of Damascus fears that Tamburlaine will slaughter everyone in his city, but his attempt to plead for mercy, sending four virgins to Tamburlaine's camp, fails.

King of Arabia

The king of Arabia, also known as Alcidamus, is betrothed to Zenocrate before she is captured by Tamburlaine. Zenocrate prays for his life to be spared but Alcidamus is killed during Tamburlaine's battle with the soldan of Egypt, and, as he dies, Alcidamus declares his love for Zenocrate.

King of Jerusalem

The king of Jerusalem is an ally of Callapine's, and after defeating him Tamburlaine forces him to pull his chariot.

King of Soria

The king of "Soria," or Syria, is one of Callapine's subsidiary kings. After conquering him, Tamburlaine forces him to pull his chariot until he loses strength, at which point Tamburlaine has him hanged.

King of Trebizon

Like Soria, the king of Trebizon is an ally of Callapine's who is forced to pull Tamburlaine's chariot after he is conquered. The king of Trebizon is hanged when he becomes too tired to pull the chariot.

Meander

The Persian lord closest to Mycetes, Meander councils the king on defending himself from the uprising, but he changes his allegiance to Cosroe after the battle.

Menaphon

Menaphon is the Persian lord closest to Cosroe. He is key in the conspiracy to overthrow Mycetes.

Mycetes

Mycetes is the king of Persia from the opening of part 1 until Tamburlaine and Cosroe overthrow him. He is a weak king whose speech is characterized by repeated sounds and clichés.

Although he complains that his brother abuses him, he does nothing about it. When Tamburlaine discovers Mycetes attempting to hide his crown on the battlefield, an absurd attempt to ensure that no one will steal it, Tamburlaine lets the king keep it until he wins the battle.

Olympia

Wife to the Captain of Balsera, Olympia is a resigned but shrewd woman who watches her husband die, stabs her son, and then attempts to burn herself on their funeral pyre before Theridamas prevents her. Then, rather than submit to Theridamas's romantic advances, she tricks him into stabbing her in the neck.

Orcanes

The king of Natolia, or Anatolia, a region slightly larger than the Anatolia of present-day Turkey, Orcanes is a fierce enemy to Tamburlaine. He has more vocal power than most of Tamburlaine's other enemies, and he is a somewhat more complex figure as well, actually paying tribute to Christ because he believes that Christ was responsible for his victory over the king of Hungary, who broke his Christian vow of peace with Orcanes. After Tamburlaine enslaves him, Orcanes curses Tamburlaine with insights such as, "Thou showest the difference 'twixt ourselves and thee / In this thy barbarous damned tyranny."

Perdicas

Perdicas is Calyphas's idle companion, with whom Calyphas is playing cards before his father stabs him.

Sigismund

The Christian king of Hungary, Sigismund makes a vow by Christ to maintain peace with Orcanes, but his advisors persuade him to break the vow and attack Orcanes while they have the opportunity. When Sigismund has lost the battle and lies dying, he repents of this perjury and begs for Christian forgiveness.

Soldan of Egypt

The soldan of Egypt is Zenocrate's father. He despises Tamburlaine for stealing his daughter and invading his land. After Tamburlaine conquers his armies, spares his life, and gives him back more than his former territory, however, the soldan praises Tamburlaine and consecrates his daughter's marriage.

Son

The son of the captain of Balsera is a brave young man who allows his mother to stab him in order to avoid torture at the hands of Tamburlaine's army.

Tamburlaine

Majestic and eloquent, with the ability to conquer not just kings and emperors but the audience of the play, Tamburlaine is one of the most important characters in Elizabethan drama. He is the source of the poetry that made Marlowe famous, and he can be both captivating and repellant because of his brutality. The key to his character is power and ambition, of which Tamburlaine has a superhuman amount, as well as the willingness to use any extreme in order to be triumphant. Unconcerned with social norms or everyday life, Tamburlaine views himself in relation to the gods, and Marlowe uses him as a tool to ask philosophical questions such as what is the furthest extent of human power and accomplishment, and whether this is significant in comparison with heaven.

Tamburlaine begins his life in what Marlowe calls Scythia, a region north and northeast of the Black Sea, and rises to power first in Persia, subsequently conquering much of North Africa, the Middle East, Eastern Europe, and India. Marlowe's work concentrates on his battles with Turkish emperors and their subsidiary kings, whose territory at that time included much of the Middle East and North Africa. Tamburlaine's personal life is closely related to his outward conquests; he wins his wife by conquering her father's kingdom and then devastates much of the Middle East in his fury over her death. He sees his sons entirely as military leaders and murders his idle and slothful son

Calyphas after he refuses to fight against the Turkish armies. At the end of his life, Tamburlaine is unsatisfied with the extent of his conquests. His thirst for power is unquenchable and, as his son and heir Amyras emphasizes, none can match Tamburlaine's power.

Like most of Marlowe's protagonists, Tamburlaine has a complex relationship with the audience of the play. He inspires a mixed reaction because he is brutal without bounds yet simultaneously passionate and glorious. Elizabethan audiences would be particularly offended, as well as somewhat titillated, by the presumptuousness of what they would consider a heathen—although the historical Tamburlaine was a Moslem, Marlowe shows him burning sacred Islamic texts and generally speaking as though he thinks of the gods in ancient Greek and Roman terms. This emphasis on mythology is also significant because Scythia is the area traditionally believed to hold the mountain to which Zeus chained Prometheus, a Titan who is famous for stealing fire from the gods and who, like Tamburlaine, dares to challenge Jupiter and the other classical gods.

Techelles

Tamburlaine's close companion, Techelles is an ambitious military leader entirely loyal to Tamburlaine. He came with Tamburlaine from Scythia and continues to be a skillful general after Tamburlaine makes him king of Fez, North Africa.

Techelles's devotion to Tamburlaine, including his willingness to slaughter the virgins of Damascus and drown the population of Babylon, reveals Tamburlaine's power as a leader.

Theridamas

The chief captain in the Persian army, Theridamas is sent to kill Tamburlaine but instead becomes his loyal and lifelong companion. Telling Tamburlaine he has been, "Won with thy words, and conquered with thy looks," Theridamas quickly becomes one of Tamburlaine's three closest advisors and most able generals. Tamburlaine makes him king of Argier, in North Africa, and Theridamas is critical to the sieges of Balsera and Babylon in part 2. At Balsera, Theridamas falls in love with Olympia, the wife of Balsera's captain, and stops her from throwing herself on her husband and son's funeral pyre.

Tamburlaine calls Theridamas majestic when he first meets him, and it is clear from part 1 that he is a valiant and powerful Persian lord, although he is perhaps not as power hungry as Techelles and Usumcasane, since he says in Act 2, Scene 3 that he could live without being a king. It is when he threatens to rape Olympia and gullibly accepts her magic war ointment over her "honour," however, accidentally stabbing her, that Theridamas is revealed to be a warrior at heart and not a lover.

Uribassa

Uribassa is Orcanes's ally and a viceroy of an unspecified Turkish territory. He and Gazellus are viceroys for Callapine while the emperor is Tamburlaine's prisoner in Egypt.

Usumcasane

Usumcasane is Tamburlaine's close companion who, like Techelles, comes from Scythia and is so devoted to Tamburlaine that he is unable to comprehend Tamburlaine's death from illness.

Virgins of Damascus

After hearing their pleas for mercy on their city, Tamburlaine has the four virgins of Damascus slaughtered and hoisted on the city walls.

Zabina

Zabina is the proud Turkish empress of Bajazeth. She tells Zenocrate before their husbands go to battle that she would make her a slave, so at first the audience feels little sympathy for her when she is made the servant of Zenocrate's maid. However, after Tamburlaine tortures her and her husband, keeping them inside a cage, and she and Bajazeth kill themselves, Zenocrate and the audience pity them and feel astonished at Tamburlaine's cruelty. Before she goes mad and kills herself, Zabina reveals herself to be a practical person by urging her husband to eat and stay alive, hoping that at some point they will be freed.

Zenocrate

Daughter to the soldan of Egypt, Zenocrate is captured by Tamburlaine at the beginning of part 1, and she remains with him as his concubine, and then his wife, until her death in part 2, act 2. Initially, she resists Tamburlaine's romantic suit and calls herself "wretched" because she is forced to remain with him, but by act 3 she has fallen in love with him and is swept up in the glory of conquest. Zenocrate is dismayed by the prospect of Tamburlaine making war with her father and her people, however. Her most difficult moment comes in part 1, act 5, scene 2, after Tamburlaine's brutal siege of Damascus. Distraught after seeing Tamburlaine slaughter four innocent virgins, she then comes upon the bodies of Bajazeth and Zabina, who have killed themselves because of Tamburlaine's cruelty. Nevertheless, she wishes Tamburlaine victory over her father and her former betrothed, Arabia, praying that their lives may be spared.

Tamburlaine's frequent superlative descriptions of Zenocrate's beauty and divine nature reveal Zenocrate's critical influence on the actions of the play. Tamburlaine's conquests in part 1 are closely related to winning Zenocrate, and in part 2 are largely a result of lamenting her death. These eloquent speeches, however, do not necessarily shed light on Zenocrate's true character or her struggle, particularly in part 1, of allegiance between her lover and her people, which is also a struggle between brutality and peace. This struggle resolves after the Soldan agrees to Zenocrate's marriage with Tamburlaine, although in part 2, act 1, Zenocrate wonders when her husband will finally cease his bloody conquests. Also, Tamburlaine's struggle with his son Calyphas, who is completely uninterested in war, is an extension of the conflict between peace and war in his mother's character.

The New Human

Tamburlaine, with his cruelty, his ambition, his tremendous capacity for violence, and his intense passion for his wife, represented a new and shocking type of hero for late sixteenth-century audiences. He was the equivalent of what audiences today might consider a Romantic hero—a passionate male obsessed with war who defies convention and whose fervency goes far beyond what is even conceivable for most people. Audiences were not even necessarily intended to understand Tamburlaine, such was his shock value and his capacity to break through the very fabric of society with his ceaseless conquests and unquenchable thirst for power.

Because Tamburlaine was a new type of hero, conquering the traditions of restraint and mercy with his passion, eloquence, and power, he challenged the traditional morality system that pervaded London theaters in the early Elizabethan period. Unlike the conventional plays that preceded *Tamburlaine the Great*, Marlowe's work does not consist of a simplistic didactic, or morally instructive, lesson emphasizing that humans must adhere to a strict and traditional moral code. Instead, the play attacks the philosophical problem of humanity's relationship to the universe and provides an example of a new and extreme worldview that seems to ignore traditional morality. It is Tamburlaine's conviction that he is as powerful as a god, and he refuses to see himself as an impotent human in a massive, oppressive universe. He believes that he can control the world and is tremendously optimistic about the possibilities of human achievement.

Marlowe does not straightforwardly advocate this worldview; Tamburlaine's relationship with the audience is complex, and he often inspires repugnance and alienation. However, Tamburlaine is not simply an anti-hero whose worldview the audience finds persuasive solely because he is a devilish figure of temptation. Tamburlaine is likely an exhilarating figure, in part, because he represents a passion that the audience is meant to admire. The play challenges the idea that humans are locked into an oppressive moral system and suggests that a new type of humanity is possible, which will break through these boundaries. The Renaissance movement in continental Europe stressed the emergence of a new model for humanity, open to diverse types of knowledge and entirely new ideas, and Tamburlaine was a vital contribution to the development of this ethos in England. Although Marlowe raises the possibility that he has gone too far, Tamburlaine provides a compelling case for a new type of human.

Power and Ambition

One of the play's principle themes is conveyed in its depiction of excessive cruelty and ambition, the characteristics that define its main character and make him controversial. In fact, the theme of power pervades nearly every aspect of the play, from Tamburlaine's conquests, to his role as a father, to his relationship with Zenocrate. Tamburlaine's military brilliance and his ability to carry out such horrendous acts—such as slaughtering the virgins of Damascus and drowning the population of Babylon —are the results of these character traits, as are his eloquence and rhetorical power that convince Theridamas and others to join him. Marlowe's audience could be expected to find such excessive displays of power un-Christian and even repulsive, as well as to find themselves somewhat captivated by it.

Ambivalent reactions to these themes extend to the other aspects of Tamburlaine's life; the audience is asked to ponder whether the hero's extraordinary passion for his wife is actually romantic love or a form of perverted possession and desire. They must judge whether Tamburlaine is justified in murdering his own son because that son is weak and lazy. Tamburlaine is generally unwilling to place his love above his military ambitions (although he does spare Zenocrate's father). He often seems to perceive Zenocrate as a treasure to be won, such as in his initial declaration of love for her, when he describes her in terms of great wealth and power. Similarly, he views his sons solely in terms of their courage and fortitude, and he has no regrets about stabbing Calyphas because he was too slothful to enter a battle.

It is possible that Marlowe implies, according to the conventions of a tragedy, that Tamburlaine's downfall occurs because of the excessive appetite for power that is his tragic flaw. If this is the case, Tamburlaine's and Zenocrate's illnesses and deaths could be seen as a punishment from the heavens for Tamburlaine's presumptuousness. This is not necessarily clear, however, since there is no great evidence that the illness involves any divine intervention; in fact, God does not seem to interfere with human affairs in the play. In any case, Marlowe poses provocative questions about the place of power and ambition in society, the desirability of these characteristics in an age of tremendous artistic and scientific advances and the evils that can result from an excessive display of power.

Topics for Further Study

- Tamburlaine is famous for arousing a mixed reaction in his audiences. What was your response to his character? Were you, like Theridamas, "Won with [his] words?" To what degree did you find him cruel and barbarous, and at which points did you find him cruelest? Is Tamburlaine a hero and a protagonist? Why or why not? Discuss the reactions you think Tamburlaine is meant to inspire. How are these reactions important to Marlowe's goals in the play?

- Marlowe's *Dr. Faustus* (1594) is also about a power-hungry character who inspires ambivalent reactions in the audience. Read this play and compare it with *Tamburlaine the Great*. How are the moral themes of the plays similar? How do they differ? What does *Dr. Faustus* imply about one human's relationship to the universe? How does this differ from the implications of *Tamburlaine the Great* ? How do the plays differ in style and form? Which one sheds more light on today's society, and which one would you rather see performed today? Explain your choices.

- Identify the key scenes in

Tamburlaine the Great, including the most eloquent scene, the most daring scene, the scene with the most important turning point, and the scene most crucial to establishing Marlowe's major themes. Support your choices with examples and quotes, and explain your decisions. Then, perform one of these scenes with your classmates. Think about the best way to portray the scene according to the point it is trying to make, and think about which characters are most important to the scene and how to emphasize their importance. What is the best way to deliver what Ben Jonson called "Marlowe's mighty line?" How can you approach your performance of the play to best express what you consider to be its meaning? Use your answers to improve your performance.

- *Tamburlaine the Great* departs substantially from the actual history of the Mongol warlord, Tamerlane. Read a prominent history book about Tamerlane and discuss how this changes your view of the conqueror. How does the contemporary view of Tamerlane differ from Marlow's portrayal? How might Marlowe's play be different if it treated Tamburlaine as he is depicted in modern histories? Support your answer with examples and discuss, more broadly, the goals of history texts and how they differ from those of historical fiction.

Style

Blank Verse

In his prefatory tribute to the first folio edition of Shakespeare's plays, Ben Jonson cited (though in deference to Shakespeare) "Marlowe's mighty line," and critics tend to agree that Marlowe's innovation in verse was the first and most influential predecessor to the stylistic achievements of the era. It was *Tamburlaine the Great* that made this powerful verse style famous. Marlowe stresses in the prologue to part 1 that it is his intention to depart from the "jigging veins of rhyming mother wits," or unsophisticated rhymes like those of a mother giving silly advice in the form of a jig, of his predecessors. Instead, Marlowe wanted to create a work of high philosophical ambitions and powerful, "astounding" verse.

The poetic tool Marlowe uses for his "mighty line" is blank verse, or unrhymed iambic pentameter, which is a meter with five beats of two-syllable units called iambs. This style, adapted from Greek and Latin heroic verse, was developed in Italy before Henry Howard, Earl of Surrey, introduced it in England. Marlowe was perhaps the chief innovator to instill blank verse with emotional force and rhythmic eloquence, and he was also influential in skillfully suiting his characters' temperaments to the nature of their lines.

Tamburlaine's lines, for example, are not just musical and eloquent but extremely powerful and majestic, with hard consonant sounds and decisive, accented peaks and flourishes, while those of Calyphas and Mycetes rhyme ineffectually and repeat sounds frequently, to no purpose.

Rhetoric

Although Tamburlaine's speeches may sometimes sound overwrought, in Elizabethan England they were fine examples of rhetoric, or the art of speaking and writing effectively. Marlowe does not follow the strict logical rules of classical rhetoric, which was used in ancient Greek philosophy but, like the ancient Greeks, he does use language as a powerful tool to convey the truth and to be persuasive. Marlowe's compelling and insightful use of comparisons, his evocative diction, or word choice, his startling imagery, and his ability to incorporate his words into a compelling and musical rhythm of speech combine to create some of the most powerful examples of rhetoric in Elizabethan drama. Elizabethan audiences might sometimes find Tamburlaine pompous, but his rhetoric is the dramatist's chief tool in portraying Tamburlaine as such a captivating figure.

In addition to their usefulness in winning over the audience, Tamburlaine's powers of rhetoric are critical to his military triumphs. Tamburlaine's rhetoric compels Theridamas to join him and allows him to inspire his soldiers to victory. Also,

Tamburlaine relies on rhetoric to win over Zenocrate and instruct his sons in the arts of war. Of course, he supports his rhetoric with his majestic looks and forceful actions, but this style of speech is the key means by which he is able to communicate his power. Marlowe saw rhetoric as one of the most important keys to power and truth. He disdained the low comedy and clichéd rhetoric of previous dramatists. In fact, he wrote such grand and forceful speeches that writers began to parody Marlowe's style after *Tamburlaine the Great* became famous, seeing Marlowe as the prime example of powerful, and sometimes ostentatious, rhetoric.

Elizabethan England

When Queen Elizabeth I succeeded to the throne of England in 1558, the nation was poorer and less powerful than the continental powers France and Spain. England had been torn by internal religious strife between Protestants and Catholics, and was quite unstable. Elizabeth, an adept and shrewd monarch who surrounded herself with pragmatic advisors, presided over a period of increasing power and prosperity, making peace with France in 1560, defeating the Spanish Armada in 1588, and garnering relative peace with Catholics and Puritans. England was not without its problems, however. England enjoyed a sometimes precarious political stability. Elizabeth narrowly survived a number of assassination attempts that would have resulted in a fierce battle of succession since, despite pressure from Parliament, she never married or produced an heir.

In this environment of relative tolerance and stability, the flourishing of the arts in continental Europe spread to England, and the late sixteenth century became famous for an extraordinary flowering in literature known as the English "Renaissance." Writer and statesman Sir Thomas More, and poets Edmund Spenser and Philip Sidney, were among the key figures in developing "humanism" in English literature; this involved the revival of classical literature and an emphasis on individual humanity instead of strictly religious themes. Marlowe was perhaps the first major innovator in humanistic English drama, however, along with his friend Thomas Kyd. Marlowe was also very influential over Jonson and Shakespeare, whose writing came at what is generally considered the height of the English Renaissance.

Tamerlane

The conqueror Tamerlane, known in Europe by this corrupt version of the Persian "Timur-i Leng," or "Timur the lame," was a fearsome military leader, famous for his brutality and his devotion to Mongol-Islamic religious practices. Born in Ulus Chaghatay, an area in present-day Uzbekistan, in 1336, Tamerlane was a member of a Mongol tribe that had converted to Islam during his father's rule. He was a thief and brigand during his youth, attracting allies and preparing for his bid for leadership, which was at first unsuccessful. After he built an alliance with the neighboring prince Amir Husayn (marrying his sister to fortify their relationship), Tamerlane was able to drive all other serious threats to his control from Ulus Chaghatay. Husayn and Tamerlane then became involved in a leadership struggle, and Tamerlane laid siege to Husayn's city, allowed a local warlord to kill him, and took four of his wives as concubines.

Compare & Contrast

- **1400s:** Tamerlane rules his vast territories by allowing his soldiers to keep the booty from the conquests and filling his treasury with ransom money extracted from conquered cities.

  1580s: The Ottoman Empire, at the height of its power, controls most of Tamerlane's former territories and arouses fear and misunderstanding from Christian nations.

  Today: The Middle East, which is the primary location of the events in *Tamburlaine the Great,* contains a number of prosperous nations with rich natural resources, but it is one of the most politically unstable regions in the world.

- **1400s:** England is in the midst of the Middle Ages. Henry IV has just come to power, having deposed his cousin Richard II, and he will deal forcibly with the insurrections and other problems resulting in part from the devastation of the Black Plague in the mid-1300s.

  1580s: Elizabeth rules England with shrewd pragmatism and, although her treasury has been overstretched by military expenses, she creates a stable environment for trade.

Today: Tony Blair is prime minister of England, and his tenure has been characterized by center-left economic and social policies, as well as his alliance with the United States in a pre-emptive war with Iraq.

- **1400s:** The Americas have yet to be discovered by Europeans, and Native Americans live a traditional way of life that varies by region and civilization.

1580s: The most brutal Spanish conquests of native populations in South and Central America have largely come to an end, but English and French colonialists have yet to establish the firm hold that will lead to the widespread displacement and massacre of Native North Americans.

Today: In the United States, Native Americans struggle with poverty and a lack of appropriate resources on reservations, but the Native American population is not becoming fully integrated into mainstream culture and does not necessarily desire to do so.

By 1379, Tamerlane had suppressed a series of rebellions and established sole control over Ulus

Chaghatay. Partly to keep other warlords in his control, since they would be under his eye as a subservient army, he then began a series of extremely successful conquests into neighboring lands. From 1386 to 1388, Tamerlane invaded Persia and Anatolia but afterwards was forced to return to defend his homeland against a former protégé called Tokhtamish. Tamerlane finally defeated Tokhtamish in 1390. After two more years spent defending against enemies from the north, Tamerlane invaded Iran in 1392, where he installed his sons as governors. In 1398, he set off for India, where he sacked Delhi and murdered 100,000 Hindu prisoners. In 1399, he campaigned into Syria and Anatolia, defeating the Ottoman Sultan Bayazid I and taking him captive in 1402. In 1405, Tamerlane was preparing for an ambitious conquest into China when he fell ill and died. He had established no sustainable infrastructure, and his vast empire rapidly decayed after his death, despite the fact that he nominated a grandson as his successor.

Tamburlaine the Great, particularly in part 2, contains a great number of historical inaccuracies and alternative representations, partly because there was a limited amount of historical information available at the time and partly because Marlowe did not always interpret that information correctly, but mainly because Marlowe's dramatic goals differed from the historical reality. For example, since Marlowe likely did not conceive of the work in two parts, it was necessary to use events prior to Bajazeth's demise, and, in the case of Orcanes's defeat of Sigismund, nearly fifty years after it, in order to form a coherent drama in part 2. Also, the play's depiction of Bajazeth and his wife's enslavement inside an iron cage stems from an alternative reading of the historian Arabshah. Other examples, such as Tamburlaine's love for Zenocrate, are entirely fictional, and reflect Marlowe's desire to cast the play in the manner most effective for developing his major themes.

Critical Overview

Among most successful plays of the Elizabethan era, the two parts of *Tamburlaine the Great* captivated audiences with their eloquent rhetoric and powerful verse. Although they remained popular as pieces of literature, they were not frequently performed in later periods and are infrequently performed in the early 2000s in comparison with Marlowe's other works. The grandiose wars and conquests of the plays may not translate well to the modern stage, but the work is now, and has been for centuries, a prominent subject for stylistic and thematic literary criticism.

Marlowe's reputation suffered because of the numerous scandals surrounding his private life, including the circumstances of his death. Claims that he was an immoral atheist and blasphemer initially affected the critical evaluation of his plays. The dramatist's critical reception recovered, however, and *Tamburlaine the Great* became one of the principle subjects for critics interested in the development of blank verse and the style of Renaissance drama. Most critics consider it extremely important, if not the most important work, in developing the style that came to a height around the turn of the sixteenth century.

Regarding the principle thematic meaning of the work, two analytical views eventually emerged to explain Tamburlaine's ambivalent character. The first view stresses that Tamburlaine is a brutal and un-Christian tyrant whose power and ambition is reprehensible. As Roger Sales points out in his 1991 study *Christopher Marlowe:* "Tamburlaine's rise to power is usually at the expense of a series of legitimate rulers. Might is shown to triumph over right." The second main analytical view stresses, instead, that Tamburlaine's glory and majesty inspire the audience to recognize the highest limits of human achievement—a view that J. W. Harper calls "romantic" in his 1971 introduction to the plays: "the view that he is a perfect symbol of the Renaissance spirit and the spokesman for Marlowe's own aspirations and energies." Harper stresses that the first view—that Tamburlaine is a "stock figure of evil"—is more accurate than the "romantic" view. But, like most critics, he acknowledges that there is some truth to both interpretations.

What Do I Read Next?

- Marlowe's *Dr. Faustus*, first performed in 1594, concentrates on a forceful and eloquent main character who sells his soul to the devil in exchange for knowledge and power. It is one of Marlowe's most sophisticated achievements.

- *Tamburlaine the Conqueror* (1964), by Hilda Hookham, is an eloquent account of the historical Tamerlane and a thorough, definitive treatment of his career.

- Shakespeare's *Henry V*, first performed about 1599, deals with an ambitious and charismatic king who penetrates further into France than any other English monarch. It is an example of further accomplishments in elegant rhetoric and blank verse in the years after Marlowe's death.

- In addition to his plays, Marlowe wrote a number of poems including the delightful *Hero and Leander* (1598), a treatment of the ancient Greek story of two lovers who can meet only when Leander swims across the Hellespont strait.

- Chelsea Quinn Yarbro's *A Feast in Exile* (2001) is a popular historical vampire novel in which Tamerlane the conqueror captures the Count of Saint-Germain, a vampire, during

Tamerlane's siege of Dehli. Tamerlane keeps the count in his service as a healer.

Sources

Jonson, Ben, "To the Memory of My Beloved, the Author Master William Shakespeare, and What He Hath Left Us," in *William Shakespeare: The Complete Works,* by William Shakespeare, edited by Stanley Wells and Gary Taylor, Oxford University Press, 1988, pp. xiv–xvi.

Marlowe, Christopher, *Tamburlaine the Great: Parts I and II,* edited by J. W. Harper, Ernest Benn, 1971.

Sales, Roger, *Christopher Marlowe,* St. Martin's Press, 1991, pp. 51–83.

Further Reading

Battenhouse, Roy W., *Marlowe's "Tamburlaine": A Study in Renaissance Moral Philosophy*, Vanderbilt University Press, 1964.

> This book provides an analysis of the play as a didactic and conventionally religious moral statement, in which Tamburlaine is meant to be a figure of evil.

Eliot, T. S., "Christopher Marlowe," in *Selected Essays, 1917–1932*, Harcourt, Brace, 1932, pp. 100–07.

> Eliot's discussion of Marlowe's style is one of the most influential modern critical evaluations of the dramatist, and it includes an analysis of the verse in *Tamburlaine the Great.*

Manz, Beatrice Forbes, *The Rise and Rule of Tamerlane*, Cambridge University Press, 1989.

> Manz offers a useful historical account of the Mongol conqueror.

Ribner, Irving, "The Idea of History in Marlowe's *Tamburlaine*," in *ELH*, Vol. 20, 1954, pp. 251–66.

> Ribner discusses Marlowe's classical sources in *Tamburlaine the Great* and argues that the play denies the role of providence in human history.

Rowse, A. L., *Christopher Marlowe, A Biography,* Macmillan, 1964.

> Rowse's book is a colorful and controversial biography addressed to a wide audience.

Lightning Source UK Ltd.
Milton Keynes UK
UKHW01f0656161018
330624UK00010B/387/P